I hope you f-
something lovely
here —

Gianna

Moonflower

March 2019

In praise of *Moonflower*...

"Like secrets whispered in ordinary rooms, Gianna Russo's important first book unfolds in the small, quiet spaces that make up a world. Cast in a rich, painterly light, these poems are manifestations of dark burdens laid bare and promises made and kept, a place where the angels of memory and the earthly pull of the body intertwine. Mysterious, tender and profoundly human, *Moonflower* heartens and astonishes with poems of unwavering beauty and strength."
    —Silvia Curbelo, author of *The Secret History of Water* and *Ambush*

"*Moonflower* is a book of loss, and of resilience and recovery, from depression, divorce, children leaving home, a mother's death. The moonflower blooms at night, and so do these poems, with an uncanny and luminous glow."
    —Dorianne Laux, author of *Facts About the Moon*

"In these "simple pages, brimming" with "rambunctious consecrations," Gianna Russo allows intimacy, genuine and guileless, to inhabit each poem, her nuanced voice ranging from "the mathematics of *bereft*" to the intoxications of the ordinary, "an absinthe of the air." Whether reassessing a lover's tattoo or the death of her mother, Russo writes from all aspects of personality so that the poems resonate with vitality: "I... rise and shake out / the waist-length hair of my soul, / and it sets all the bells to ringing." *Moonflower* is rife with such splendid and passionate animations."
    —Michael Waters, author of *Parthenopi: New and Selected Poems* and editor of *Contemporary American Poetry*

"For decades, Gianna Russo's passion has fueled the flame of poetry in the Tampa Bay area—as writer, teacher, editor, publisher, and general cheerleader. We've long enjoyed her poems in magazines, and listened to her marvelous and musical readings, so it's a pleasure at last to hold these poems collected in *Moonflower*. Russo's poems are both tough and sensuous, and like most powerful poetry, are essentially hymns filled with longing and love for what is, what has passed, and what might have been. 'The blanched lip of the fruit bowl,' she writes, 'kisses nothing but motes of dust.'"

—Peter Meinke, Poet Laureate of St. Petersburg, FL, and author of *Lines from Neuchatel, The Contracted World: New & More Selected Poems,* and other books

"In *Moonflower,* Gianna Russo lets the world be the world, without judgment, without apology, without sentiment. That's a rare thing, an act of bravery and compassion. What a pleasure it is to discover a poet who can do that."

—Jay Hopler, author of *Green Squall*

"How clarified the images of this world, these lives inhabited by the strife of sunlight, of bog and forest, of harsh light shone on relationships that interweave like the southern vines of Florida, of anywhere we are in our complicated lives. These are poems that illuminate the tendrils of what it means to be alive and sharing. Welcome to the writing of Gianna Russo who aptly evokes the giddy scent of orange blossoms to persuade us to keep on living in this tangled world."

—Nicholas Samaras, author of *Hands of the Saddlemaker*

"For all its music, Gianna Russo's poetry's most startling aspect is a fearless, haunting, dark elegance. Poem after poem, she faces down the shadows and contemplates the spells and omens Nature trots out. Moonflower is a beautiful, very serious collection, long-awaited."

—Philip F. Deaver, author of *How Men Pray* and *Silent Retreats*

Moonflower

Gianna Russo

Kitsune Books
Quality books for eclectic readers

Moonflower

Kitsune Books
P.O. Box 1154
Crawfordville, FL 32326-1154

www.kitsunebooks.com
contact@kitsunebooks.com

Printed in USA
First printing in 2010

ISBN-13: 978-0-9827409-0-3
Library of Congress Control Number: 2010935536

Front and Back Cover Illustrations and Photography
by Lou Russo. www.LouRusso.com and www.LouRussoScenes.com
Author Portrait, back cover: David Salvador

First Edition

Contents

Acknowledgments

Thanks to the editors of the following publications where several of these poems first appeared:

ArtNews: "Felon"
Bloomsbury Review: "The Artist Forrest Bess Explains" appeared in a previous version.
The Blotter: "Damselfly"
Ekphrasis: "Composition in Afternoon"
Florida English Journal: "Each Day is a Wishbone"
Forum, the Florida Humanities Council Magazine: "Angel of Drought"
Florida Review: "A Thing about Rhumba" and "An Afternoon in January"
Karamu: "Grief is Your Only Angel"
The MacGuffin: "The Bridgekeeper Notices Fall," reprinted in *Sunscripts*
New CollAge: "Felon," reprinted in *ArtsNews*
Organica: "Be"
Saw Palm Review: "Handbuilt, Thrown, Altered"
Split Verse: Poems to Heal Your Heart: "For the Sake of the Body"
Sweetlit.com: "In the Kitchen of Remembrance"
Tampa Review: "18 Degrees Inside a Cliché"
Three Candles: "This Day, Framed in Light" and "Photo of Edvard Munch on the Beach at Warnemunde, 1907"
White Pelican Review: "At the Reliquary"

"Winter Destination," "For the Sake of the Body," "The Artist Forrest Bess Explains," "Tag," "In the Kitchen of Remembrance," "Senior Year," and "This Day, Framed in Light" also appear in the limited edition chapbook *Blue Slumber*, published by YellowJacket Press.

Preface

The poems in this book span much of my adult life. During the decades I've spent writing, I've had the coaching of many wise teachers whose influence has helped me mold and shape these words. They deserve my thanks and have my gratitude.

First, a huge *thank you* goes to Anne Petty and the staff at Kitsune Books for believing in this work. *Molto grazie* also to the writers who were kind enough to write blurbs for the book: Silvia Curbelo, Phil Deaver, Jay Hopler, Dorianne Laux, Peter Meinke, Nicholas Samaras and Michael Waters.

For artistic stimulation and for the solitude in which to write, I thank the Suwanee Writers Conference, the Hambidge Center for the Arts and Sciences, and the Spoleto Writers Workshop.

I thank the word-gifted and craft-passionate writers who were members of the group we called Tampa Bay Poets in the 1980s and early 90s. We were mutual mentors to one another through our bimonthly workshop of 12 years. They taught me how to uncover gold. Some of these poets have passed out of my life or passed on, and some of them are still kicking poetic butt. I remember and bow down to all of them here, including Gayle Natale, who invited me to my first "poetry meeting," Joelle Renee Ashley, Silvia Curbelo, Charles Flowers, Susan Khan, Dionisio Martinez, Rhonda J. Nelson, and especially Phyllis McEwen, with whom I've shared 3 decades of poetic questing, poetic pacts, and blissfully wandering conversations. I also sincerely thank Phyllis for her sensitive editing of the original version of this book. In addition, two USF professors had the kindness to notice my writing and urge me forward. Though they have passed on, I pay homage to Willie Reader and Hans Juergensen, along with his delightful wife Ilse, for welcoming me into the world of poetry. I also thank Tom Abrams who gave me my first publication in his pivotal magazine *White Mule*.

My more recent tutors have also made indelible impressions with their wisdom and expertise. I send bear hugs to Peter Meinke, Poet

Laureate of St. Petersburg, FL, and his enchanting wife, the artist Jeanne Clark. They have graced me with their friendship, laughter and insight for over 20 years. Chocolate kisses go to Susan Lilley for her instant friendship, insane good humor and commiserations and to Michael Hettich for his perceptive recommendations as to how to shape these poems into a book. I tip my hat with sincere gratitude to all my former creative writing students at Blake High School and to all the poets and volunteers at YellowJacket Press. I send a special shout-out to John Fairweather for his loyal belief in my poems, and to Katie Riegel and Kate Sweeney for their impeccable suggestions regarding how to better this work. I send a life-time love-fest to my best girlfriends, Debbie, Brenda, Joni, Gail, Lynn, and Cece, who have been my cheerleaders since we were cheerleading age.

Bouquets of moonflowers go to my devoted sisters, Tina and Felicia Russo, and their husbands David Salvador and Kent Foss for their love, unwavering support and patience. A very special thank you goes to David for my cover photo. In addition, I send a long-distance bouquet to my cousin Lou Russo, and his wife Priscilla, for their gracious efforts in creating the cover image for this book.

Unmatched gratitude, X's and O's go to my parents, Joe and Belle Russo: to Dad, for apprenticing me in the fine art of telling a great story and for teaching me early on how to be awed by the things of this world; and to Mom,-- with regret that she's not here to witness this book- - for planting the seeds of poetry in me as a child by reading me nursery rhymes, singing and playing the piano, and buying for me and my sisters the complete set of Childcraft books, wherein I fell in love with rhythm, rhyme, word-play and mind-pictures before I could even read.

Finally, I humbly thank and dedicate this book to my three closest beloveds: my sons, Anthony and Frank Scaglione, for giving me such richness of heart and spirit, and for standing by me always; and to my husband Jeff Karon, my most insightful editor, my confidante, my life-mate and my love. I am forever yours in poetry.

—*Gianna Russo, September, 2010*

i.

Although the wind
blows terribly here,
the moonlight also leaks
between the roof planks
of this ruined house.

Izumi Shikibu

Angel of Drought

Something with an august thirst has drawn
up the Hillsborough as if through a straw.
A tawny tannic trickle
inches the empty riverbed.
The cattails have gone brown and brittle,
the lily pads, under some dark spell,
are reduced to the size of dimes.
Something with the drive of life-force in reverse
has stolen away our lake—
last night street dogs claimed
each shore and ran as far as I might skip a stone
before their feet touched mud.
And I can walk across the mud,
but for rank puddles where frantic fish swim
and woodstork and spoonbill trail them
like desperate refugees.
Nature trots out such omens.
Something with an itch for withered buds
and shriveled grass,
some nemesis of typhoons,
enemy of hurricanes.
Every day its draining touch
draws closer to my door.

Straight On to Zero

Maybe
the sun shoves
its torch through the sky's yawn
a century of hardwoods might
blink and be ash
while we all
stare at the lunatic
start of the century
sometimes
I'm sure
this place is forgotten
in its damned handbasket
when people wait a half-life
to carry home
a thumb of bread
a tear of milk
or maybe not
who can say
what's moral
anymore it's all sick jokes
flesh eaters and bones
under your pillow
fold it up
in the newspaper where
walls walk off in tourists' pockets
and countries vanish
what if
icebergs aren't invincible
the porch light goes
out around the world
or goes on
or maybe not

Emergency Room

All day the sun had splintered light.
It had shot through the kitchen window,

an arrow pointing at the tension
in that house, a hissing kettle, a rattling pot,

a drawer slammed so hard it split.
The slick foam of anger burbling everywhere.

You unwrapped a dull knife-set
of words, and started to throw:

butter knife, butter knife, steak knife, carver.
I slammed down a palm on the counter,

a fist, a juice glass, a jelly jar that
shattered across my love-line—

sick-sweet gush of blood and
a gash the length of the mound of Venus.

That stopped you, even though the blood
wouldn't, wouldn't stop for a butterfly bandage,

a race to the emergency room,
and a white lie even I could tell

the doctor didn't buy:
I cut it washing dishes.

You held my good hand,
held water for the pills,

stayed with me through the stitches and didn't
look me in the eye.

In the Kitchen of Remembrance

In the first inch of sunrise,
believing me asleep,
my husband slumps in his quarter
of some memory room,
weeps to ten confidants, his fingers.
This is our kitchen, this
the invented grief of his future:
orphaned, as always; newly widowed.
His fear brews this over
and over he has told me,
concocting loss and its aftertaste,
forcing on him the cloud-dark cup.

The kick of forestalled bitterness
moves his hands to become solemn workers:
he shakes fragrant beans into the grinding mill,
coaxes steam into milky foam.
He hopes I'll rise to these cues.

But if I could touch him
through constructed sorrows,
I would beg him
send the future back to bed,
since it is not my silk gown,
not his leopard robe, not the sunlight
assembling itself in *now*.

His quiet sighs steep through the lavaliere room.
Cruel or not, I lie in our bed quiet as the moon.

Photo of Edvard Munch on the Beach at Warnemunde, 1907

So painterly, pointerly in his loin cloth
       there at the edge of the gray scale.
Against the parallel lines of surfside and sunrise

his alter-ego mimics him in miniature,
       poised to dart naked off the print,
and abandon those griefs which have only

now begun to claim their grim places
       on his canvas. See how the blackness
of his shadow binds him to his subjects?

How his brush pierces the air like an arrow?
       How he poses with his palette
bright as a funeral bouquet?

Manic-Depression Approaching Spring

Off the edge
of winter, the icicle
hangs tenuous, its grounding
place diminished with late
March thrusting through.
Just a few moods back, all
was solid, was brilliant, full
of cold prisms flashing
in weightless light.

Now each wan
sunrise drains, each
helpless hour in
the same slant which
forces an outburst
of tulips, melts
to the merest
see-through
thread
of who
I was.

An Afternoon in January

A chain-mail net, the sky was, metallic
and dull, which she noticed only after
she'd replaced the receiver and looked out
over the dead back yard, the pool with its
skin of ice, the swing set turning to rust.
She walked straight to the cabinet and poured
three fingers of vodka, knocked it back straight,
staring past French doors, out over the lawn
of stiff brown blades, then helped herself into
her coat, and forced her body out of doors,
where the frostbitten air cut like oyster
shells, down across the broken lawn, across
the unbearably silent yard because
of that call, to the path unrolled along
the river, an empty footpath stretched like
a bandage along the river that lost
itself at every turn, and walked herself
through her own desolation there beside
the empty shoreline, where oysters died in
their frozen beds, and the tide pulled itself
like a cripple from shore to shore.

Handbuilt, Thrown, Altered

the Hillsborough once poured
itself sluggishly past our porch
orange blossoms persuaded night air
of what it couldn't know
breaking into gardenias and lavender
the backyard curved through crescents
of light in the crown of the door
stairs convinced themselves
of our comings and goings
the desertion of stenciled rooms and
refinished hardware   the crib
rebuilt and emptied again of milky breath
the way you turned your back
on clay and glazes   your disregard of ash
how you could sleep against my weeping
you could have lived there
how could you
wedged in the kiln of emptiness

Grief Is Your Only Angel

He stirs a finger in my broken cup:
it could be any hour,
any season stitched from this emptiness.
He pulls up to my window on the fumes of regret.

The patch of window light slides toward its bruise.

I kneel here on the vacant sill
while he shakes out his jacket.
My memories jangle in the pockets, useless coins,
mismatched keys that don't fit anything.

In my window the rectangle of violet sky
careens helplessly over our everyday—
the agony of backyard swings,
the dreadful, open gardenias.

He offers his magic wishbone,
its twin prizes: grief or gloom.
I press closed the book of my palms.
Save me is the entire text.

My window completely abandons the sky;
I'm a silhouette deepening in this ache.

He padlocks the end of opening
and leaves me with only his footprints:
one, the signature of loss;
one, the braille of good-bye.

Moonflower

In the yard anguish has taken root.
All morning, its thorny branches
scrape and scrape my window.
I pace the rooms, closing doors
on what used to be,
straightening the cupboards
where loss pools inside the cups.
The blanched lip of the fruit bowl
kisses nothing but motes of dust.

All afternoon the sun faints on its divan,
reaching thin fingers into the lemon balm.
I want to take myself out to the mulch pile.
Middle-aged, weary,
I'll lie quiet in the loam,

watch evening make its way through the rosemary.
When shadows sculpt star-points out of thorns,
a lacy perfume spills from the trellis.
The moonflowers turn their porcelain faces up
and open themselves to the dark.

For the Sake of the Body

But this is a useless ritual.
On the pillow it always rejects, I place my head
and offer myself to the sleep god,
the set punishment of denial.
I settle my back and ass onto the comforter,
which is mute and offers no reassurances.
I calm my belly into the earned slackness of a mother's body.
I take out my breasts until they are easy.
I let my feet turn away from themselves
and rest on the meager sympathies of the mattress
like both sides of the argument for my life:
the one I think I have, the one I think I want.
I uncurl my hands which have held all and nothing
and stretch out my arms which have reached for everything.
I loosen the muscles in my neck.
Between the minor consolations of headboard and footboard
I open my legs to some small goodness,
the meeting place of my hands.
Although every cell is swollen with the loss of you,
I try to lay down this outmoded will.
Still, the bedposts salute four ways to promise nothing.

Tag

When awake, I sometimes noticed
the shadow of her beard.
It was evident here, too,
in the tumble of light
which rotated our identities
as if we were a tag-team soul:
one moment I was she,
   sliding my pointing feet
   into her pantaloons,
then she was I,
   fastening my corset of bone.
Beneath the sheen of our skirt,
our hoop swayed like a skeletal bell
with me/her as the breathing clapper.

A menacing man lumbered
toward us/me/her,
his eyes blunt, milky nuggets.
He wore a future century
in his clothes.
He lunged at us like a hunter.

Up the marble staircase,
across the mahogany floor,
she/I skittered like a startled pheasant.
We were saved by a secret boudoir,
powdery and feathered.
Secure, I glided to the mirror
and found her gone,
no trace left on my chin or jaw.

Myself undid my satin jacket,

unmuzzled my breasts from the bustier.
Then the outer door disappeared.
My nipples knotted like
blind, pink fists
as he rushed in.

Felon

Right off, you knew
she was the type who could steal,
could stuff cosmetics in her pants
and walk out with a
dare-you-to-stop-me stare.
The cashiers would take a nervous swig
of coffee or a cigarette and look aside
'til she was up the road.

You met at this crazy bar
with rumors of her circling your head like smoke:
she lived with outlaws or some
twisted religious cult.
She was naturally cruel.
You were fascinated.
For weeks you fantasized about
the angle of her smirk rubbing along your belly.

It lasted awhile.
Then sometimes she came very late and watched
the early a.m. staring at the tube,
no talking.
Then she wouldn't come.
She dared you to stop her.

You go on with it.
You pick at the scraps of your fantasies
like the old skin on a sore.
You haven't told a soul.
She trucks to Mexico City, tells it all,
cusses tequila 'til her memory's shot.
Swears she takes home whatever she wants.

To an Actor in Spanish Town

Your love is married and there's
nothing I can give.
You carry your hurt through Ybor City
like an empty sleeve, a broken shoe.
With all your nerves dancing
in your hands, this is not a play,
not a part you've studied for years.
You don't know the lines.

Yours is a silver face.
Thursdays, you walk Seventh Avenue thinking
of parts of Germany, of clear rivers
and wine breaking over your tongue,
stages where love is a perfect hurt.
You will take yourself to Europe like a gift.
You think you will often dance.

Days open to the empty
rehearsal of her name.
Your love is married and you'll never
beg for her gift, but go
to your father's house alone.
There you kiss your hurt where
it tastes like your lover.
You know the part.

I would show you how impossible
is this dance, how parts of your blue
saxophone are shining like gifts.
But your lover's married
and although some dark
girl in this city is breaking
open her rose,
she isn't me.

Bitch

Her coat drops off in clumps,
the mangy bitch.
I hate the way her skin shows through,
a pocked and oozing map.
She's not going anywhere.
I've locked her chain to a steely spike,
staked it down in the infernal earth.
I've given her chain twice the length she deserves.
But you see what she's done:
clawed every bit of green to dirt
and left me with this shredded lawn.
Even the weeds are gone.

I hate the way she digs and digs
for the bone I never gave.
She howls and whips around that stake,
scratching out the furrow of her heat.
Sometimes I want to beat her.
I grab my belt;
she bares the ice picks of her teeth.
We have our little face-off,
but neither one gives:
I stomp into the darkened house;
she growls and bites her leg.

Sometimes she whines and whines with thirst
until I go out and thrust my face in hers.
I smell the pure flame of her breath.
I spit in her throat.
I would slice a bit of fat
from the back of my arm
to please her gut,
but you see what she's done:
what dangles from my shoulder
is all that's left.

Someday I might undo her collar,
chase her to the street.
Then I'll walk back into a life alone
with just this stump bumping my side
and the negligence of my heart.
She'd be a different animal running free.

But right now I can't bear to let her go.
Not while I can rip the fur from her skin,
then nurse each wound
with such fury, such devotion.

Poetry Stood Gazing out the Window

since I had turned away, heartsick
and fed up. Months before storm
season, she stood motionless, transfixed,
searching the Gulf for the green flash all
through oppressive August.
I didn't care.

As a child, I had closed my eyes
and thought about the alphabet,
the swift slide of the K,
the silver swing of the H.
These and their dozens of cousins
had been my recess all my born days.

Now the saucer of my heart had crusted up.
I claimed it didn't matter,
all those *no's* muttering amongst
themselves in the other room,
with a sound like envelopes closing.
All I had left could have echoed in an inkwell.

When two white birds of paradise crashed
one upon the other,
I stared from an empty doorway.
Then the fuse boxes blew and I thought
the turquoise flash might mean luck.

As hurricanes pummeled the playground,
Poetry stood at the open casement,
too starry-eyed to turn aside as the hours shattered,
too stupid to pull the shutters.

Approaching Infinity

In a landscape of catastrophe
how much can you subtract from joy?
Can you halve it like an animal,
hang it in the gloom to dry?
Hardened and bark-like,
will that afternoon in summer
with sugared ginger and figs,
will that gift of honeyed hours survive?

Sorrow tunnels the heart like termites
and grief opens its blue parasols
into the gloaming.
But that evening in autumn,
plump with lamplight and wine,
twines a section of itself
toward what still might be.

This world means to quarter bliss,
slice it to a sheer fraction.
Yet figs grow round from the thinnest curve
and bees tending their simple house,
take death for what it gives
and line a bed for birth.

ii.

In the sky without limits,
Only the moonlight stays.

Zhou Xuanjing

Each Day Is a Wishbone

My boys are born for this:
dew christening their bodies these fall mornings
when school is yesterday
and grass is their friend.

They swing into warm afternoons,
take their bikes to the street
and slay it with speed.

My life is full of their rambunctious consecrations:
one of them spits straight into the sky;
the other blesses the rose bush with piss.
All life threads the dirt at the backs of their necks.

I marvel how they've braved this fractured season,
with the family they had last year carved up, gone.

In deep evenings they sleep toward school days.
When I check and tuck covers
close to their moving dreams,
I fill myself with the wafers of their breath.
I was born for this,
their warm living smells—
sugar, salt, yeast.

Posy for an Empty Garden

There were no ivory orchids.

On this first anniversary we will not celebrate,
I drove without chauffeur to our wedding place.

I brought two yellow roses.
Our future was not present.

I wore no crown of stephanotis;
there was no lace.

I wandered through the garden
where the arbor does not stand,

followed my loss around the pool
where flagstones rest in earth naming

lilies   violets   baby's breath
rosemary   dill   mint   iris

I stood before no one in the sacred spot
where grass and leaves are as they were.

A witness only to fallen moss,
the October sky shone as purely blue.

I retreated up the aisle which is not there
and gave away the memory of *I do.*

This for pure remembrance:
one rose I twined through the wrought-iron gate

which was not flung wide by any promise.
The other I gave to the statue of Saint Francis.

The years that I would give to you were absent;
the past, admitting nothing, my sole attendant.

Autumn Pantoum

Dawn carries morning to the threshold of sky
and mist becomes one with the heartbroken streets
of Asheville. I may come to forgive you,
or else abandon myself to the art of grief,

to mist, breaking the one heart of each street.
How is it trust tumbles into sorrow,
like an abandoned bride left to the start of grief?
Once your hands were a gloved tenderness,

a trust. My tumbled sorrows
recall the autumnal light of your eyes,
how your hands were gloved in tenderness.
They touched softly, even when placed over my mouth.

In the autumnal light, your eyes
sought any altar beyond me. You'd rather witness irises
touch softly, rather place kisses in my mouth
than hear how our vows were forsaken.

I sought altars beyond you, witnessed myself in your irises,
a silenced clapper in our wedding bell.
You would not hear of our forsaken vows,
cleaving only to ceremony, a wind's assurances.

Both a silence and a clatter of wedding bells
echoes down the years. It is autumn; what's past
is cleaving, ceremonies, wind, and my only assurance
that healing will somehow cross over such mountains.

Echoes. Down the years, it is always autumn, what's past.
In Asheville, I may come to forgive you,
healing me, and somehow crossing the mountains
where dusk carries evening to the threshold of sky.

Hibiscus

At twilight, day pushes its rowboat from shore.
Cardinals begin keening in the orange trees,
pinning notes to the score of what might have been.

All night I arm-wrestle shadows.
I leave my bed in exile,
seek one island for these thoughts,
one plump pillow for memory.

The moon, like a tugboat,
drags day to another port.
At dawn the jaybirds mock the dark.
Outside, morning mist wears a gardenia scent
and the red hibiscus crowds my door,
its crown lush with ruby stars.

Reverse and Move Forward

My car lost hold
began to roll backwards down
the hill, while I stood apart from
the propped door in something
resembling panic or awe
and watched it slip back, slide
down despite its brake, taking
the slope
      slowly,
            then faster,
                  then urgently,
as if it wanted
that going down, needed it like some
lesson of transformation, a way
to live backwards, not exactly
traveling into the past
but something parallel,
how everything could mean
the reverse of what we believe,
like a one-way street that drives
better when you take it
wrong, the car flying
downwards as if
it were built for this

and we don't know
the truth about pain, the stop
sign which might really open
on the other side at the perfect
destination, as if all
we have tried for and couldn't
grasp has been a way
of getting to start, as if the engine
knows this, idling backwards without
resistance, letting go to the force

of wheels and gravity, while
the steering wheel resigns
itself to life with no visible
driver, and the seats
plump themselves into the satisfaction
of being empty.

The Bridgekeeper Notices Fall

Like a stranger from up river,
     a tourist without a map,

wind stumbles through the cattails
in a dappled, amber light.

The bridgekeeper smokes—
puffs out little clouds
wondering if he can fill the sky:

     his days pour over the river dam,
     his years spill over the bridge.

Mullet flash up into the air
in a slanting, hyacinth light;

     a bum walks off with the tags of his coat,
     a child searches for her gloves,

but the bridgeman only listens for his boats
and turns to the sun setting over the river
     like a man turning back for his sweater.

Senior Year

Even though I keep my window open,
when I call to your youth, it ignores me.
It dashes down the street,
reaching for luck's strong-arm pass.
It leans against your truck where the motor
warms itself with possibility.
Your youth hands back the allowance
I try to sneak into its pockets.
It mows the grass unasked,
bursts onto Fridays with its own cashed check.
Your youth is collecting appliances and pans,
forks to spear a wish, knives sharper than my anxiety.
Your youth refuses to call home
when I need to hear its voice.
It resists any curfew and instead,
long past bedtime, introduces me
to the way these rooms are sighing,
the murmur of wind's regret,
the evening sky commencing its sure-footed retreat.

Damselfly

Paused on the underside,
the damselfly folds her wings across her back
like two matched slivers of isinglass.
Her body, thin as a thorn,
flits by in sepia tone.
She pins her wish to the ridges of a leaf,
then flickers along the edge of a pond,
the night-green mirror of her fairy life.
Her sorrows are wind and a stream gone dry;
she lets herself be blown from sight.
In late day sun, when her wings glint like tears,
she darns the torn hopes of the hyacinth.

Thursday Night Poetry

The night of the Cuban cigars, the room
we ravished with poems tilted on its one good corner,
that dingy corner where the smoke was legendary and
the wineglasses smudged with our best lost lines.
In the one livable room in that house on Platt Street,
our wet shoes huddled with the shadows of our feet
tucked inside. The smoke was an absinthe of the air,
green fairy gifting us with the words we lived for,
the new ones, quivering on the pages in our hands,
each with its island of breath.
After every fresh verse the night turned ravenous
for talk, there in the silent country of the one livable room.
We roused all our beloved poets from their slumber,
and summoned them through empty doorways,
spreading rumors about certain rhythms,
debating the coup of each line break.
We stood metaphors in front of a firing wall:
some escaped with their lives; others crawled off as similes.
This was every happiness we could imagine.
In the word-crammed dust,
the smoke was a nosegay of Old Havana.
A window peeped out on the nefarious alley,
and the porch pondered the drugged-out underbelly
of the bridge, before the neighborhood grew tulips
and strode off in its Brooks Brothers suits,
before Platt Street unraveled into years leading us
                                    away from then, then, then.

No More for the Moon

The one magic dare
all my friends
have made love to—
month after month
you present your opaque belly
for the licking.

You beguiled me too,
each of us smuggled home
your trophy of closet lust
until, among ourselves,
the same hackneyed secrets
turned you up
like a pat of butter on a line,
like cream splashing our pages.

I've vowed to ignore your nightly self,
but my milky body
builds, relinquishes
its monthly nest to your cycle
like an obsessed cliché;
you are sleeping like a seed
in my dark tilled patch.

Though your quarter's
a luminous slice of melon,
and plumps up harvest full,
orange as a halved cantaloupe,
I'm through winking on paper
at your one blank eye.

This time
I'll steal off while you're new:

When your helium face
grins into my hair,
I won't look back.

Poses in Natural Light

Would you mind, he asks, spreading
a bolt of chiffon into the nimbus of afternoon.

A seduction of light.

The penumbral walls of his studio.

A clutch of women, each a silver *fleur de lis*
picked for his camera's imagination.

Disrobed and serious, I posture their same curved breathing.
They are the bouquet I would leap into
instead of this question of my belly,
my breasts bloomed beyond themselves.

As if my body were a firm stalk.
My body is incandescent with age.

The charcoal percentage of afternoon.

The penumbral walls of his studio.

His face is new with the filament of want
and I'm myself as I am wrapped in nothingness.

The Artist Forrest Bess Explains

I close my eyes and paint what I see
on the screen inside my eyelids. There,
hieroglyphs of amazons and birth times,
of craters like a matriarch's lost places,
of yellow stars and shallow stones
tremble in the rushlight before dreams.

For years I thought they were dreams.
I denied them, set them to sea
in my place of forgetting. But like skipped stones,
they never floated far. There
on the border of sleep, they'd wash up, placing
themselves time after time

into ebbs and flows outside of time.
When I could no longer ignore their dream-
shine, I began to paint. There was a place
in Bay City, a spit of land from which I could see
the world washing itself. I lingered there,
discovering the tides of stones

and hollows together. My life was a blue stone
weighted in a time
lighter than bone. There,
I was woman in one dream,
man in the next. No one could see
the two were inseparable as a name and its place.

I knew I was tracking the immortal place.
The days I handled like dull stones,
but at night I could see
the perfect androgens and their time-
less language rising to me. I dreamed
and found my dark canvases plastered with their

world. They were leading me there,
transforming my manhood to an open place.
The woman in me stepped from her dream,
finally. Her vision was a clear stone.
We imagined moons and were beyond them, leaving time
in its fistful of earth and sea.

I have learned my place. In this time,
I cut my colors in stone. The coordinates of dreams
shine up from the sea. We are taking you there.

Where Heaven and Earth Are One

Above the adobe: clouds, a flambeau.
Against night space: a rushlight whelk.
Here a shoreline condenses in radiance.
There dunes dissolve beneath zodiac light.
   Think of white paper and printer ink.
   This black & white is about black-and-whites.
Corona of sunrise, nimbus of belly,
scintilla of thighs, throat-lit hollow.
Nipple and aureola:
mountain ascending its shadow.
   Everything could be something else.

You in Your Metaphors or Craftsmanship

Your mouth is full of what you will never say.
Words float up through your stillness
and catch in your voice-box,
a vessel freighted with promise:
        I would, I want . . .

In your speech of starts and finishes,
everything unsaid eddies
in the syllables of your body
and comes only to itself,
like a wakened man discovering his own hands:
        I will, I wish . . .

Months from now, words will push
themselves onto paper,
holding out their shy arms
like a love unasked for;
words will spring from your hands
and swim away to do your deeds.
Watch them leap into munificent sunlight,
the flood of every silence.
Here, the simple pages, brimming.

Said

Picture the sky thinning into breath.

When I said *blue* all the multiples of water unfurled.

When I said *secret*
cocoons clung to my ear with their fleeting tales.

I thought *listen*
and the milkweed pods burst into an overture of begetting.

I traced a crescent, a curve, an arc.
Then palm blossoms rounded into berries
and green tendrils spiraled from stalks.

I drew a circle for the moon
and a square for the four winds.

I thought *No*
and death shrank itself into a blood-red seed.

I lifted one finger. I imagined the word *Now.*
I closed my lips and made my mind a pearl.

Then the ocean settled around me like a shawl,
and my bosom was flooded with sunrise.

For Any Reason

Because winter birds crowd together on the shore
like newcomers at a party.
The river is amber smoke coiling
into what's left of the hometown.
Because everyday the countryside
gets elbowed farther back.
Because of clouds.

Because you've fallen in love with your husband again.
Your lover uncorks the champagne.
The baby has colic and there's no relief.
Because people you know have erased themselves.
Because your son asks you, *What is rape?*
Because of AIDS.

Because the 21st century stammers at the window.
The torturer gets handed his next assignment.
All the world is pitching its shackles into the square
or soldering new ones.
Because you don't believe calendars
and planets are all there is.

Because jazz and the blues decode you
and the alphabet that erupts is sweet pain.
Because sometimes hurt has its compensation.
These are the *whys* you can say
of those you can't.
Because brown eggs cradle beautifully
like wishes in your hands.

Be

    Light
is a porch light
is a dark house ringing red light
is the red pair of Chinese shoes
the hand with a pair of queens
the man from Queens who wanted to sing
is a slow singing when you lose
a Cadillac ashtray full of loose change
the forgotten change of clothes
how you can't forget the breaking cup
the sound of an oar breaking open the lake
is Great Lakes Erie, Superior
the eerie noise in a widower's house
an Inuit house huddling over its oil
two miners huddling over their lungs
is what love is like in an iron lung
is a reason to set the iron down
is a prison full of reasonable men
the prisoner's lawyer getting a stay
is the safest place to stay in Gdansk
the biopsy results which say you are safe
the first thing your sister will say to you
the first slaughtered whale and the northern lights
is Saint Nick and Claus and the shop in the north
is every saint and every whore
is every Russian dance before snow
is snow like another lost color
a color as quiet as the last doe
is the *do re mi fa so la ti*
is the star ray of the smallest blue dwarf
is the starry, Starry Night
is the good night, the sleep tight
is the good god
    is the God
    Is

Winter Destination

This imagining of your distant slumber

how a battery of light pours into winter
dawn, washing itself on the coast
where you lie curled

even in this unreachable city, the restless shuffle
of your breathing proclaims itself to me
in sleep, which is beyond
the fact of never having
shared your sleep

how our bodies always desert us to the light opening
all around, so that we move bewildered
as tourists through the strange
mansions of age or
illness or sex

I would love you past all boundary if I could once
see your eyes flitting beneath the lids
of dreaming, only once, your mouth
open to the stories of sleep
like a child's

Last Summer Home

The two of you, teen
years like tattoos of honor
on your shoulders, the truck
squealing off down late-night
streets, away from blue beds where
your sleep awaits and even now is a warm,
even breathing. The first-light hours of summer
jobs are nothing more than a slight pestering buzz.
Wedged between you, a sweet girl, someone's
blond first love whose heart will surely be
pounded raw by its desire, like the
hip-hop thumping the dashboard.
Ahead, the grand billboard: *Adults!*
Adults! Such beckoning flashes
as you reach the curve
and gun it.

Bridge

A latch hinging workday to serenity,
metaphor flows lucid and wandering beneath it,
disguised as a river.

Connection curves into simile.
Disguised as sky, archetype floats above.

Pretending to be handrails, the girders,
laid out like runes, forecast passage to things good.

Planks form a simple analogy:
as goodbye is to waterfall, welcome is to grass.

Now unlock the symbol of where you begin.

iii.

Now I carry images of moonflowers with me everywhere

Jesse Millner

Bats at Twilight

I've heard how they claim the Congress Street Bridge:
    like folded fur handkerchiefs
        hundreds hang on the underbelly.
At dusk they swoop out to sport
    and poach and cloak the sky
        in a great wolfish exodus
of instinct and appetite.

    Once I saw dozens darting
        in lava lamp shapes among sky scrapers.
One moment, the vertical space was jammed
    with only air and traffic sounds,
        the next was spelled with their loopy cursives,
their dark Morse Code.

    I recall how I roamed with my new love
        through a magnolia labyrinth.
We watched a pair of bats knit air,
    needling the unraveling light.
        Even as shadow and want called us home,
they braided and plaited whatever was to come.

Morning Apart in Appalachia

Dove-colored sky announces your absence. This is a Quaker day—
plain, doing without. This vista is a prism splitting you
and me in its refraction, or a silvery blade that pains just for now.
This clean hurt is its crimson trail where flesh parts into throbbing.

Mountains spear the sky. The way clouds absorb their tips, I am
carrying you inside me, the meal of you in me already.
I have eaten your banquet before and before. This moment you
are becoming my bone, my tissue, my mucus, my blood.
My nourishment, you are feeding me unstoppingly.

Mist whitens the dells below.   At dawn, I wrote *You Love Me*
in the hard-packed dirt, the earth which will give way to frost
and a grave sky. But for now, it stands, clear as a kept promise.
My heart flies, raven-like, over the mountains.

Man Napping

An illuminated letter, an S
in the white space of the bed
where tiredness is an excuse two hours long,
begins the story of his body, a worn
theme that moss beyond the window dreams
in gray scarves, monotone. A silver
scarf which his mother places over her up-do
Saturday mornings, leaving the beauty
parlor. The long-lost brother makes an appearance,
drugs still snaking up his arms, his war
in Korea like a pop-up picture
in the background. The sister, with her page-boy cut
and a cigarette cupped in her barmaid's hand,
mouths words the man can't hear, of what he wishes
she might tell him, but won't.

Sighing in his chest, the man, still asleep,
puts his head on the rough desk where
his boyhood carved its name. Inside a cloakroom,
the shadow of his father looks at him
with one eye only, since the other
is a glass ball he pops out each night
and polishes like a pearl, but the one real eye
is so hard to see into, so hard to read
that when Father dies somewhere
between *Daddy* and *I Love You*,
the man who isn't even a man yet
feels cleaved in his balance and stumbles
always afterwards as if without an ear or a foot
in that absence of forgiveness.

Just before he wakes, as sunlight
stripes the room through half-closed
blinds and a prism in the window,
the man's dream becomes his grandmother, fresh

from the paper factory with a whistle chirping
in the distance, or it could be cardinals
in the man's own orange trees since the afternoon is
fading like old ink and the man is still
as a comma on ivory linen, while the color
curls around him in a thousand years of light.

Composition in Afternoon

Light climbing through the window on its pale ladder,
light tossing its yellow cord to the floor,
light opening its butter-colored robe
which slips from blonde shoulders
into a pale yellow pool in the corner of the studio,
light removing its lemon-colored gloves
so I can write for the first time
in the presence of another soul,
light polishing its lenses,
light polishing each solemn corner
until there is nothing between my love and me,
just these two rooms holding my sorrow, my breath,
a bed of Prussian blue still as a drenched boat,
this patient desk poised for my next command,
light stirring gold petals into the bowl,
light pressing the pensive chords,
the odd notes of this page I am writing,
light and music, words and love lifting me
into a different life,
light stepping out of its saffron-colored shoes,
climbing out of itself, out of everything

Blind Knife Trick

You're abandoned by all the old know-how.
The spoons' eyes stare dull as cataracts,
the long balancing poles have lost their grace.
And whose blank plates are these,
and how will you set them in orbit?

You don't even recognize yourself,
the gypsy who used longing like a flourished scarf:
whenever you clapped your hands someone disappeared.
Or came back.

Now you're the one conquered
by love's sleight of hand.
You display empty pockets
as if to discover your self-confidence,
but it's all beyond you now:
impossible to imagine forks bending under your touch,
the piked tines curling up.

You lick the indiscriminate tongue of the butter knife,
fondle the hatchet blades as if conjuring their power.
Even the butcher knives you've mastered
seem to squirm with their pointed lives.

You tie on the blindfold, hold your breath:
the air shimmers with something genuine.
Now fling the knives,
hear them whistling like birds of prey
into your perfect aim.

18 Degrees Inside a Cliché

The garage attendant licks his knuckles of ice
and we descend into the purgatories
of a rented car, an alien map.

Nothing could make this city green,
nothing could change the contortions of
its name in our mouths,
the violent consonants and pitiful vowels.

Hunkered in weather that wrings your bones,
it's a city completely without glamour.
Even a simple breakfast is beyond it,
even easy music or a well-mixed drink.

The rivers are braced with metal.
The clouds are a burden of memories.
But our adventure is more than these salt-gray streets,
more than sky bearing our very first snow.

My bravest intentions melt into your skin
and it's no small power that summoned you here:
our ferocious, giddy need
is purely glinting in the cold.

A Thing About Rhumba

It was the 42nd year of my undulations
it was night spilling south out of borealis
the stars all frazzled
it was the second year of our second marriage
the days of naked lavender and blue slumber
it was our first year of dancing in public
the itchy moodiness of chairs around a floor
the broody nudgings of a microphone
it was a Latin trio
the interior sultriness of rhumba
it was a Morse code calling from your pulse to mine
the slight caesura of your lead
the way desire spun between us
it was the suggestion of port on your lips
it was the joke of martinis
it was the saltiness of the saxophone signed by your palm
there, at the small of my back
it was the swollen voice of the conga
it was candlelight spurning the shadows
the still-warm steps that stumbled out of doors
it was the awning clearing the constellations
the precise way we mapped the darkness of Hyde Park
the way silence navigated the street
until from an upstairs window
shutters thrown wide to night air
the curtains dazed with moonlight
it was his low needful grunting
his grunting and her moans
her question-and-answer moans
her moans like interpreters of longing
it was their cries signaling the still-point
they came to

coming beside the open window
coming beside themselves
it was you and I
it was breath and silver
holding on, listening.

At the Reliquary

Later we stood side by side under red pine,
hearing the frantic gossip of a crow,
the cathedral tolling its dead and blessed bones.

Our same breathing was a holiness
without words, without gestures.
He said, *Is there any way to improve on this?*

I thought of placing his hand on my skin,
here where it slackens and goes soft
or here where the knitted bones curve
while he lifts away my blouse
as if it were a sacred cloth.

I thought of my fingers on his hair
where the silver's come in coarse and gleaming
as the swollen moon at its perigee:

He made me stand silent and look
until I knew what it meant.
I stood there, glowing and empty,
a chalice waiting to receive its solemn grace.

Tattoo

How many years it took me to accept
that permanent blot, the ink-spot
　　　you thought would proclaim yourself.
To me, it was scar, a coal-mark, two blotches of regret
　　　placed snug enough near your jaw
to defy any starched white collar
　　　that might sail you to success.

Out of sight, you'd let a stranger's vampire needle
　　　prick a blue-grey love-bite on your neck.
When you came home newly-minted—
　　　stubble and artery, throat and ink—
I cried like a heartbroken schoolgirl
　　　into an old washcloth.
Now I touch that sooty kiss with almost-tenderness.
　　　Smudge of a heart, you tell everyone,
meaning, I guess, your heart or mine, dusky with living,
　　　besmirched with loss, blurry with love.

November Valentine

Remember the emptiness of the room, how we
        cleared a space for the blushed waiting and twilight?

Remember how we chose the lilies whose fragrance rushed
        out, and the sunflowers, the rough splendor of their faces?

Beyond an archway, piano songs stilled our breathing.
        Candles fingered the air with gold.

Your hair was braided with two ribbons, one for courage,
        one for loss, and it floated on your shoulders.

There was a sword-prayer and an altar rug.
        It seemed I stood there unclothed

        as you called down all your ancestors.
You wore a silken happy coat, with jade trees for fortune.

Remember the birds of paradise,
        how gingerly we hung the lanterns?

iv.

No moon-talk at all now.
Only dark listening to dark.

Carl Sandburg

First (Born)

February 15, 1956

In twilight sleep my mother
      lay moaning while evening
slid out from afternoon
      winter and one heavy breath
possessed another, the heart-and-flower
      day contracted sideways
and pushed itself down the month's
      middle, faster and harder through
her royal-blue sleep, bearing
      down past anticipation,
past the needle of midnight, and she
      panted through the pain as
her girlhood slipped from the room, her future
      donned its most delicate gloves and
waited to catch her body's pure
      word, a metaphor for *she*
herself, my breath a *yes*
      in a parenthesis of blue volts

*"Sometimes they'll wait to pass until you're out
of the room."*

Hospice nurse

So it was, in that mere
half-hour before dusk when we
walked ourselves from her room to nibble on an
early supper and Dad was telling us about his train ride
to Tampa, the journey that, like a compass needle, would
lead him into the next 50 years, as we had a few laughs over
his Navy days, the before-I-was-born days,
his storytelling ordinary as any Sunday

And this was after the priest who converted her
told me, *She's already going,*

Her dearest cousin stood next to the pitiful bed,
stone-faced, steady as a surgeon, and said, *Goodbye, Belle*

Her best friend kissed her head and listened
to the rasped rumble of her breathing, how it pressed on
with its work, like rough pistons laboring in a ruined engine,
or like someone drawing a dull buzz saw across a laurel—
once, and then pausing
once, and then pausing—

The priest from South America administered
last rites in his quaint, accented Latin and flicked
the holy oils on her, foot and crown, and twice from her
death-dream she hummed a response, a murmur-grunt that
said, *Yes, I hear,* so that even I, deserter of the church,
could see her spirit flutter like a pinwheel
in that mere slice of time
before we stepped out.

The Right Dress

I grab the hand of my sorrow
and walk into Westshore Mall.
The light is fake and flood-like,
a white-silver current sluicing through
the Food Court down to Macy's, past
the makeup counter, up the escalator to Better Dresses.

What do you wear to your mother's funeral?
Black, gray, black-and-white, the mannequins nod.
I only have an hour to find no shimmer or flirt or décolletage
or lace. There are business casuals and empires and sheaths.
It's the wrong occasion for mark-downs; I need something exact.
But in the dressing room, only weariness stares from the mirror
until I sit in my old bra and underwear on
the little corner shelf under the security camera.

I might see her in Better Dresses,
holding out a hanger with something
pretty enough for death. Or is she holding
out a flame? Is the rack of ugly dresses just one long silver
boat and am I trying on ways to launch it into the vastness
of this day? Yes, fingering these dresses,
we are lighting the pyre together, until
I make the choice that will push her
toward the western light spreading out there
in the parking lot, gold-rose and dove-gray.

First Monday without My Mother in the World

Two days ago we were clinging to the wisdom
of the hospice nurse,
each word a life raft she helped lower down
from my mother's pain.

The night before she died I had roamed
the corridors at Hospice House
and seen the man in black trousers and black coat,
head shaved, face tanned, taut and muscular as a Doberman.
There in the wee hours he chatted up the night nurse
while he wrote and wrote in the white notebook on her desk.

I walked past the vacant lunchroom
and sat without tea or crackers,
just sat in the dimness that opened the cave
where I could close my mind away
from my mother's death rattle.

Now it's a new week.
Instead of saying what it's like, new motherless morning,
let me tell about my grandparents' graves,
how my one sister called to say, *Let's take the flowers there,*
and my other sister said, *I can't do it. I'm done.*
So just two of us went out and found
the plots at Myrtle Hill, Section 3.
We set out bells of Ireland, and examined the dates.
We set out lilies, daisies, roses
and my sister swept the dust away.

Or let me whisper how this morning I woke my husband
and moved him over me so I might weep a bit,
because I can't really get to it, can I,
though this was to be all about Mom and this first Monday

and here I am,
still trying to talk about the black-hole feeling
of starting the week without her in the world,
as if it were some portal to a perilous land,
and God knows how I'll wander there,
even old as I am, already more than half a century.

See, right when I saw the morgue man
leaning towards the nurse in the dead of night
with his fake lick-your-hand ways, I knew
he would track me into a poem so that I couldn't shake him,
and here he is, pushing the stretcher with its black,
bunched garment bag belted down on top,
zipped and ordinary as a satchel,
and I'll be damned if I can look away
from his jaunty step and his wolfish face
as he props back the door at 2 a.m. and shoves,
shoves out his cargo.

Meditation to a Crystal Bowl: A Long Slow Train

Through a meadow of tall grass, unlike any meadow I've seen, since such meadows no longer exist, I saw-heard in the distance a circle of sound that began to hum and moan around the rim of a crystal bowl being played by a woman who asked us to close our eyes and let our minds go wherever they would.

Mine went to the meadow and to train tracks, and before long there were many rail cars hooked one to another, and to the locomotive, all a far-distant caravan on the edge of seeing. As the scraping and whining of steel wheels along the track wheezed on and on, the train approached me through the high grass.

I stood, a lone figure on the platform in the middle of my mind, and I willed that train to me through the swaying grass. I willed it knowing that when it arrived, the doors would open and the only passenger would be my mother, dead only two weeks.

I lay in the dusk of the meditation room, while the sound of wheels and rail revolved and I wished and wished. But it was difficult. The train was not meant for my direction. With every halting yard of track it seemed to hold itself back.

Still I willed it to me, urging it to shift course and bring to me my mother. But the more I wished, the slower it came, as it if the engine itself hated moving that way, and at last I saw that I should stop wishing.

So I thought, *you can go*. Instantly the train reversed direction and headed away through the meadow. The waving grass covered over it like a green-gold tunnel. It made me cry to watch it and the sound went with it.

Hawk

I heard her crying from the ancient oak,
the tree where a hive of bees
had set up shop huge as a fruit crate.

Eating lunch on the veranda did I see her
drifting on the updraft?
I'm not sure, but I could hear the hawk
announcing her intentions like a magician.

Weeks earlier I had walked beneath the sister oak
as three work men stared up at resurrection fern.
When I asked, they pointed and there
I saw the nest, high as a wish.
Moments later she swooped up through the branches.

The day I heard her cries pierce the afternoon,
I thought how she'd kept her house there all those weeks
and wondered about her chicks.

In the meantime, someone had stolen away
the bee hive: not a keeper who cut it away from
the high trunk and carted it off to some safe haven.
No, it was the bug man, with his poison stick.
The bees rained down by the hundreds on the sidewalk,
and their honey-casket got thrown in the trash.

This day, I heard the hawk's hunting lament,
but didn't see her, no, until *thunk!*
The antique brick and glass of our building
shivered in summer stillness and a brown rag
somersaulted from the second story into the flower bed.

I rushed to the edge of the porch
and peered into the bushes.
She lay there shuddering, on her side,

one wing at a fluted angle, eyes open, feet stiff.
I ran to stand over her—
called animal control, got a wrong number,
flagged down a stranger who told me,
Stay back, she just stunned, she could take your face off!
But then she stopped.
I bent in close and saw her stilled breast.
Above, the window held a mirage
of summer sky and cumulus.
And this whole time I'm thinking,
It's three weeks today that Mom's been dead.

Empty Porch Chair with a Mountain View

All day you can look out on the loveliest nothing.
The morning vista is a smoky bluest, bluer, blue.
The nighttime sky is a wreath of stars.

You sat here for hours, lost in the laurel green.
My favorite place to be, you said each summer,
and each autumn, when the valley unfolded
its yellow-red counterpane.
It's just three months, Mom, since your death.
When everyone else had gone to bed,
you'd claim this luminous solitude, a frosty beer, a cigarette.

Now the porch planks moan as we step
to where your absence huddles like a stunned wren
in the turquoise Adirondack.

Whatever It Takes

The methods of torture used by the Inquisitors had five stages. Each stage was meant to evoke fear. If the prisoner didn't give in at one stage, he was moved on to the next.

First, you were merely threatened with torture.
I'm sorry to have to tell you
the results of your lab work.

Next, you were shown the instruments of torture.
This is the radiation room.
This is the chemo pump.

You were undressed and prepared as if to be tortured.
Please take off your clothes.
Put the gown on so it opens in the front.

You were tied to the instrument without actually being tortured.
So, you want a second opinion?

Finally, you were tortured.
You may feel a little pinch.
Lie very, very still.

My Favorite Curse Word

How mortified my father was
to hear my mother let it fly.
This was a word for sailors and roughnecks.
He should know:
he came of age among Navy men,
Catholics and Italians—
the triple whammy of great cursers.
But he never cared for swearing—
too crude and low class.
Even when his hulking anger boxed our ears,
we never heard him cuss.

My mother was a different story.
She'd been brought up a Southern lady,
daughter of an attorney and Methodist to boot.
She spent her girlhood helping her mother
Host teas for the DAR or sewing bees for the church ladies.
But she left home for Tulane
and settled herself in a girls' boarding house
while she went to school. There
she learned to smoke, drink bourbon, eat oysters.
On Miss Annie's moonlit veranda,
you were just livin' large when you swore.

Decades later
she'd roar with glee at the dirty joys
of her Tom Lehrer records, her favorite.
George Carlin's seven words sent her into hysterics
and she adored even staid James Lipton
on Actors Studio, asking
What's your favorite curse word?

*   *   *   *   *

Fuck the cancer that pummeled her for years

in a triple whammy—breast, mouth, lung—
before it took her to the mat.
Fuck the chemo, the 5-day-a-week torment,
       drip, drip, drip, drip, drip,
water torture as cure-all.
Fuck the vomit, the balding
that left her girlish curls
whimpering in the drain.
Fuck the knife that hacked off
half a boob and half an underarm,
fuck the way she stood before the dressing room
mirror with her mother-of-the-bride gown
raised over her head and a grim smirk stitched
where her nipple should be.
Fuck the radiation chamber
where my mind took a snapshot fit
for Amnesty International:
my mother strapped onto a table
thinner than her back,
balancing all of her 70 years on that ledge.
Over her face, they placed a mesh mask
molded to fit to her very skin,
then screwed the mask down and imprisoned
her face inside that cage.
They aimed their lasers at the infinitesimal spot
on her tongue that was killing her.
Then they shot it with their death-ray.
Everyone stood safe in a concrete cell of mercy
while my mother lay inside the dungeon
where her fear teetered, screwed to a plank,
and she counted slowly to two-hundred and forty, slowly
until it was done.
Fuck that.
Fuck the doctors, even the ones who cared
and tried so hard to help, but especially
the last one who hardly knew her
and took the pictures inside her,

then called her family into a private room,
so that even before you went in you knew it was bad.
Fuck how, later, he wouldn't take Mom's hand
and just looked at her bed sheet when she asked,
What did you find?
and fuck how he left me to her asking,
Am I dying?
and fuck how I didn't say no and I didn't say yes.
Fuck those goddamn nurses who insisted on getting
her onto the toilet while she moaned and fell faint,
and insisted on turning her in the middle of the night
until she screamed,
Help me!
and wanted to turn her again
though it was obvious she wouldn't live
long enough for bedsores.
Fuck them.
Fuck that stupid one in particular who
kept turning on the light.

*   *   *   *   *

These nights when I'm in darkness,
I can hear her voice skipping through the moonflowers,
tipsy and laughing with her best gals.
Coming off months of chemo that shrank her down,
stole her taste buds so everything
she swallowed turned to chalk,
she'd got herself blasted on one glass of wine.
I'm drunk, she's giggling,
I'm having a ball.
Let everyone know.
She's laughing now.
Call up the whole family.
Put it on the internet.
I'm drunk, I feel great.
I don't give a fuck.

Sorting Her Clothes

We eye the shoe boxes she's stored so tidily,
so organized with her notes
written in black marker on the ends:
grey boots   sparkly heels   black pumps (new).
She grins at us, standing
the way we've seen her a thousand times
in that ratty robe and worn down slippers,
sans make-up, hair sparse and dull.
She's thinner than any of her girlhood,
but her eyes still hold that gleam of mischief,
that heading-toward-a-chuckle look, the personality
that got her crowned "Wittiest" way back when.

All this from the photo propped on the pillow of her bed.

My sisters and I juggle the boxes off the highest shelf,
open them, slip our feet into her footprints' shadows
and remember: *these she wore to your wedding and*
these to yours. She still had them!
And so many handbags—metallic gold and black satin—
so many corny purses sporting seagulls
and leaves and patchwork.
We don't touch *that* purse, the one she carried
when she left for the hospital and never came back.
It sits on the nightstand shunned
for its lipstick, breath mints and keys,
near the overnight case still packed with her last days.
All the rest we place in piles:
for ourselves, for her friends, for the mission.

Next we grab armfuls of what's hanging,
and the size range is a testament to suffering.
One or two dresses still there in 1X, her healthy years,
for she'd always been a big gal. Then 18's, then 14's
and how thrilled she was to be wearing a 10—

One good thing that's come out of this, she'd said,
and a few new size 8's. In this green moo-moo,
she cooked a hundred Sundays' worth of macaroni.
This rose blouse she wore on her 45th anniversary.

Last we wrestle open her dresser drawers,
where her intimates confess all:
the bras she cut down and took up as she shrank and shrank,
the left cup with a false mold she'd stitched in by hand;
the pads for her underwear, the small box of Depends.
And back far in a corner, bitter evidence:
with its flip-up lid and cigarette rest,
a blush-red ashtray to cup in her palm,
tattle-tale ashes sifting inside.
It stops us fast and we can't go on.
Despite the second closet, there'll be no more tonight,
it's too much already as we lug things away.

Mom's watching us do this.
It's a start, we say.

Eating Truffles on Thomas Wolfe's Grave

"The last voyage, the longest, the best"

Gingko trees tinge the avenues in verdigris
all the way to the edge of Asheville.
Our old friendship has been a half-silence
that spread into distance.
But today we're reunited with Michael.
Amidst the pebbledash houses and staid B & B's,
we're easy again in his buddha ways, his raffish heart.
He's taking us in hand, strolling us down hilly drives
as he points out what's homespun and historic—
the old sanitorium where Gilded Age tuberculars
came for a cure; the grassy lawn where
Highland Hospital blazed to cinders and took down
Zelda Fitzgerald, darling of the flappers.
Smoke over the hills now, and isn't it all?
My own mother's gone just since spring.

There are iron gates alongside the French Broad River,
87 acres, dogwood, poplar, and
here's poor Thomas Wolfe tucked in the ground
more than 70 years at the Riverside Cemetery.
Michael wants us to lie head to head on the grave
while he snaps a shot. But no, we think not.
We won't lie still, despite the ruined days of our past,
not since it's summer and we're friends once more
and we stopped before at Chocolate Fetish.
We'll sit laughing next to the Wolfe family plot
and share luscious puffs of cocoa and lavender,
something rare as caviar.

v.

Not the moon. A flower
on the other side of the water.

Denise Levertov

The Littles

So much depends upon three banty roosters
chuckling to themselves in the mock orange
sunrise that peeps in from East Tampa.
For weeks I walk off mourning as dawn feathers the sky
and the roosters begin their bugle calls:
one perched in the weeping willow,
one roosting in the live oak on Violet Street,
one scratching on the shore of the pond
we call Lake Roberta.
Puffed up and acting put-upon,
they set up their crows like pinballs
and fire away, one to the other to the other,
full throttle blasts that zing
across pond, brick streets and bungalows.
    You, you are you!
            Blue, blue are you?
    Who, who are you?
And I'm wondering that myself, balancing grief
like hand weights, as these orange sprays of spunk
pull back the plungers of their throats
and let those morning shout-outs fly.
Scrawny and struttin' like they're somebody,
they are littler than the cats,
not bigger than a breadbox,
full of themselves, boasting their black
tail feathers to the ducklings,
the blue jays, the lizards ruffling their red neck scarves
as I walk round and round the pond,
counter-clockwise, to the before-sad,
inside this triangle of neighborly crowing
that's just plain funny, the arrogant little things,
prancing 'cause they ain't afraid of nobody,

trumpeting,
> *Who are you, you?*
> *You are who, who?*
>> *I've got the whole mornin' in my voice.*

After the Argument

Autumn flip-flops like a caught fish
and the winter solstice unfolds its long bolt of night.
This world is a basket of sorrows.

I cried and cried when they drove off so fast.
What were a few bruises to them, when they didn't mean it,
when the way stretched clear as a ball-field

and ruin seemed as impossible as snow?
Now, in they come, my sons, striding into *What's next?*
and showing me how quick we can turn back to love.

Live oaks to my winter, pearls of my breast.
They trek over this earth with daybreak in their hands.
The locket of my mother-heart unclasps in happiness.

Daylight Savings Time in Mid-life

Morning creeps up dark as sinkhole.
Last night we lost an hour—precious,
when each morning brings a new stiffness to his knees,
a long twinge across my back.

From our bed we can see the dazed garden,
overhear the cardinals chirping to each other faithfully.
The strewn bedside magazines claim 50 is the new 30.
Poll finds senior couples enjoy more time in the sack!

Blood orange blossoms intoxicate the air
and we used to do that all afternoon,
petals scattered on the sheets,
a towel on a rug, on a sofa, in a chair.

There's a shuddering
and outside wind whooshes through crepe myrtle.
Then over-ripe fruit sounds a thud in the dirt.
Later he and I read magazines on the deck
while dusk wanders the yard for hours.

Our love clings and clings,
like hitch-hiker seeds on canvas shoes.
Spring forward, say the clocks,
and we can't help it, we do.

Lucky Arrival

Late, but not enough to ruin us,
we coast in from the brink of crisis.
Not just the worn engine worries us.
But when you stroll out through tides of grass,

your smile like a lighthouse,
your laugh, a rescuer's bell,
we disremember the anxiety our life is.
Delivered into your easy ways,

we step across a threshold
and marvel how each room in our heads
unlatches the moment you waltz into it:
here's the morning chair where you write in the sun,

the shadowed desk where you type at dusk.
On the table your blue bowl echoes itself,
while you unseal a jar plump with olives
like coaxing open a fist.

Your picture books line up along a wall
while a favorite vase atop a shelf
unfolds into eucalyptus.
Our visit drifts on orange blossoms, wine,

the grey-day stories of before we knew you.
The scenes on your painted fan open the afternoon:
the round harbor of friendship,
the moorings good fortune has steered us to.

Gridlock, with crepe myrtle blossoms

The workweek swelters into happy hour
and I'm stuck in the rush, the bottleneck
of a turn lane, the whole southern vista
smothered in SUV's and faded Lincolns.
All across the northeast sky, weather
beats its breast, coal-dark and clotted.
I'm praying that my car, a three-time
hand-me-down that takes in water like
a leaky skiff, makes it to the *porte cochere*
before everything breaks over me,
this middle-age, my mother's muffled heart,
my sons' truant phone cards, and you, my love,
with that stitch in your side that doesn't quit.

I'm still trapped in the inside lane between
hurricane season and drought,
my hands are stuck at 10 and 2,
saluting news radio's war dirge
when the wind picks up
and shuffles the air, ruffling pink and purple frills
on the crepe myrtle next to the drawbridge.
And slowly they float across 3 lanes of traffic,
not enough pay, overdue bills—
the fringed mauve pinches of frou-frou, adrift.
Though nothing budges and the sky's at half-mast,
all at once my windshield is awash with happiness.

This Day, Framed in Light

The room is a vast impermanence,
mere sea mist and Atlantic blue.
The desk dreams of Van Gogh; the dresser disrobes
for the mirror. Fuchsia, orchid, scarlet, bronze
light carousels through passion fruit and traveler palms.
Beneath a canopy of black net the bed is white
as wedding cake. Icing sheets that fold and melt,
slide inside the breath of you.
The room froths around painted mermaids,
sure of themselves as eels.
The windows quiver with voodoo.

I'm aware what betrayals are hooked to our bodies.
I wonder what frightful visions you own—
like the vanity wrestling its usual nightmare
of turpentine, razors, boxes of paint.
Those times when your eyes fret beneath wakeless lids
as if Vincent were toying with your own ear.
Or as if your mother were mouthing your name
futilely and finally through cancer and morphine.
You thrash in a sarcophagus of memories
where passion fruit hang like distinct regrets.
There is no way for me to soothe you at such times.

But this day your slumber stretches out like so much joy.
The room is shabby and temporary:
mere walls, an impression of sunflowers.
Operatic voices bloom in from the hall.
Light tumbles across the exhausted garden
as you open to sleep, a museum of god.

Only

Singly I flew and happiness was my giraffe.

—R. Vazirani

My charmed fox, my netsuke,
you are always next to me,
since our long-off solitary days when
no one else on our street knew
how the nonchalant ruins of luck
had left us both so bowled over,
so utterly given to climbing fences,
and to charting blue maps towards angels
and strange philosophies.
How we had both memorized
the ghettos of naked moments and
the mathematics of *bereft.*
Your frustration was a poor, front-yard astronomy,
a rolled-up copy of *The Skeptic.*
I'd spent my pocket change on loss.
But life sometimes opens like
a fold-up altar and there I saw
watch fob, rock garden, mustache comb, Japanese sword.

Loyalty, sometimes I wonder
as we gaze through the telescope of together,
what magic power let us transform this suburban devotion,
fan-shaped and glinty as an Alaskan skinning knife,
to an ocean incense that has scented us both to the bone?
My ink stone, our little buddha life is like
an ancient glittering text, translatable only by desire.
When you surrender your body to gypsy dances,
there is no other man to feed me asparagus.
Take these nude sketches into the orange grove,
for you are my tiger beauty and
I shall never be single again.

The Fixed and Startled Way

Henceforth I ask not good fortune, I myself am good fortune.

—Walt Whitman

Now I claim my place in the ring of the moon-poets,
the champions of violets and ash
whose sleep spills on the floor
until waking shapes itself to the ribs of words,
for I am the guide of the alliterative present,
the conductor of the past in its assonance of *O,O,O*
and I gather to my bosom all the seers
of desert and jungle, all the prophets of rhumba and jazz,
I am the skyscraper stacked into clouds
and weighing down the world with its glory,
even the vultures spiraling see the gleam of sweet sun
on my eyelids and the mournful moon on my heels,
O vagabonds of the sentence,
I travel to the curved tail that instructs me to pause,
the precise dot that commands me to stop,
Red sky at morning, red sky at night,
this heart primes its conveyor belt of blood,
packaging the afterbirth of setting out,
safe return, foolhardy love-matches,
Dear breath, Dear sweat,
I lie down in my mother's body
on a sheet of swallow sticks and cardinal feathers,
while disillusionment crawls onto its mat
and regret curls into its trundle bed,
My spirit is cool water at the throat of the disheartened
and whiskey on the tongues of the daunted,
cowardice wobbles and keels over like a sad boxer,
but I myself rise and shake out
the waist-length hair of my soul,
and it sets all the bells to ringing.

Notes on the Poems

"Grief is Your Only Angel," "Composition in Afternoon," and "This Day, Framed in Light" were commissioned and performed as part of the dance concerts "Excavations: The Descent Aloft" at Eckerd College, St. Petersburg, Florida, Spring 1998, and with Moving Current Dance Company, Tampa, Florida, Spring 1998.

"Poetry Stood Gazing out the Window" borrows the title and some lines from various poems and a reading by Billy Collins.

"Approaching Infinity" is based on Peg Trezevant's painting by the same name.

"Reverse and Move Forward" is for Phyllis McEwen.

"Damselfly" was written for *In Late Day Sun: Florida Plant Life Studies,* a collaborative project with the photographer Lori Ballard.

"Thursday Night Poetry" was written in memory of Gayle Natale, Hal Mason and Joelle Renee Ashley, and is dedicated to Silvia Curbelo, Tom Ellwanger, Charles Flowers, Susan Khan, Phyllis McEwen, Dionisio Martinez, Rhonda J. Nelson, Jennifer Weaver and others who were sometimes-members of the Tampa Bay Poets in the 1980's.

"Where Heaven and Earth are One" is inspired by the work of photographer Edward Weston.

"Said" is based on Peg Trezevant's painting "Mary's Painting."

"Bridge" is after a photograph by Hannah Pagan.

"Composition in Afternoon" is inspired by "Gymnopedie #1" by Erik Satie.

"This Day, Framed in Light" was nominated for a Pushcart Prize by the editors of *Three Candles*.

"My Favorite Curse Word" is for the Great Broads (who) Read Great Books: Drew Alessi, Doria Gomez, Mary Jo Hayes, Mary Anne Ingram, Laura Preston, Gwen Romanello, Debbie Romanello, Becki Sedita, Peggy Smith, Marte Watson and Joann Weaver.

"Sometimes they'll wait to pass until you're out of the room." is for Leah Clark and Janet Baker.

"Eating Truffles on Thomas Wolfe's Grave" commemorates a visit in summer, 2009 with Michael Mann. "*The last voyage, the longest, the best*" is engraved on Wolfe's headstone to mark his death on September 15, 1938.

"Lucky Arrival" is for Susan Lilley and Phil Deaver.

"Each Day is a Wishbone," "Senior Year," "Last Summer Home" and "After the Argument" are for Anthony and Frank.

"Tattoo," "November Valentine," "This Day, Framed in Light" and "Only" are for Jeff.

About Gianna Russo

Poet, writer, and teacher Gianna Russo, has been nominated for the Pushcart Prize, received (twice) a Hillsborough County Artist Fellowship, and received an honorable mention for the Florida Artist Fellowship. She is an Arts Fellow of the Surdna Foundation and of the Hambidge Center for the Arts and Sciences.

She has had poems published in *The Bloomsbury Review, The Sun, Poet Lore, The MacGuffin, Calyx, saw palm,* and *Tampa Review,* among others. Her non-fiction essays have appeared in the *St. Petersburg Times.* A teacher of creative writing and English for over 20 years, Gianna is the founder of YellowJacket Press.

She is a lifelong resident of Tampa, Florida, where she lives with her husband, Jeff Karon.